SoulCry : book six

LOVE
FOR THE WOUNDED SOUL

an intimate poetic
expression of the deep
longings and cries of the soul

The Lord hears their cry and saves them.
He watches over all who love Him.
Psalm 145:19-20 (paraphrased)

Trudy Colflesh

Bridal Cry

Bridalcry Publishing

Colorado Springs, CO

Copyright © 2012, revised 2018 by Trudy Colflesh

Cover and page design by Nathan Fisher,
www.nathanfisher.com

ISBN 978-0-9848599-5-5

Additional Copies Available At

www.encouraginghope.com/soulcry
Amazon: Go to Trudy Colflesh books

Table of Contents

CHILDHOOD PAIN

BROKEN SEX

SHAME

DENIAL AND TRUTH

Foreword

As the reader of *Love for the Wounded Soul,* you are about to embark on a journey to your heart. This book speaks the personal, often hidden thoughts we didn't know how to speak, or are afraid to utter.

Were you raised believing your behavior was more important than you? Did you believe you had to earn love? Did you struggle with shame over not measuring up? Was there abuse in your family of origin? Do you struggle with perfectionism, unforgiveness, shame? Has sexual intimacy become distorted for you? Do you have lost memories? You may not relate to every situation, but the emotional impact may be familiar.

Read the material at your own pace. Let the words speak what your heart may want to say. Listen to your inner self and believe what you are hearing. Show kindness and understanding to yourself as you discover what you need to know. Write and meditate on the feelings that are stirred.

Allow your heavenly Father and Jesus the Son to comfort you and bring you to an understanding of truth. No matter where you've been, what's been done to you, or what you've done, you are loved and wanted.

The truth in this book will bring you healing and freedom. The enemy is defeated and you are no longer a victim. You will step into the joy of knowing you are loved and will learn to walk in healing hope.

ABOUT THE NOTEBOOK PAGES:

The Soul is expressing its deep cries
of emotion in the notebook pages.

About the Scroll:

The Lord responds to the cry of the Soul in the scrolls.

BABY RITUAL

Sweet little baby,
So cute, so cuddly, so happy.

Long ago
When no one knew,
You were the centerpiece
Of a Luciferian ritual.

You were taken to a barn,
Laid in a manger,
Wrapped in swaddling clothes.

You represented another child,
But this time the "baby Jesus"
Was mocked, not worshipped.

Sweet little baby
Decried of any power to save,
Your pure innocence
Betrayed by evil men.

You were dipped in animal filth,
Submerged in all that is ugly

And opposite of pure,
Laughed at for weakness,
No Messiah to save.

Then began the purification of being "cleansed"
Into the true religion
Of the god of light,
To grow in allegiance to the deity
Who brings wisdom
And knowledge of right.

But Jesus, a greater power,
A greater light,
Shone bright in revelation truth
That he had come to save
That small innocent babe
From chants and vows over you
To a god who was not true.

Years later, in recall
You were now free to renounce it all.
And little baby child
was washed pure and clean
By the love of her Jesus
Who came to redeem.

BABY RAGE

Baby rage!
Red-faced
Screaming, baby rage!

Don't hold me down, tie me up,
Wrap my body,
Force me to be immobile!

Who are you?
I'm scared, frightened,
And really angry!
How dare you use me
For your own perverted plans!

How dare you
Make me represent
The object of your distain.
Don't mock and defile
The Baby I will come to love.

Screaming, angry, mad!
My body covered with filth.
Your filthy hearts
Oozing out your wicked plans
On little me,
Helpless to protect.

But I can object
And scream and cry
And identify years later
With all the emotion
That is justified

Of baby rage.

FLAMES OF ANGER

Red hot flames
Of anger!
And why not!?

With the door of denial
Unlatched from a raging furnace
Of unprocessed, lost memories,
A survivor discovers
An unknown fury
Of anger!

It's wrong, all wrong!
Babies, toddlers, children
Tormented, tortured, killed.

Perversions, rituals
And every evil imagination
Of the heart,
Perpetrated on the unprotected
And innocent.

Hidden away in every victim
Is burning a fire of anger,
Kindled and fanned with each assault
Against God's child.

God's child is kidnapped
Into Satan's kingdom
And only as God ransoms
And rescues,
Is this little one
Free to feel the anger
Of abuse.

So spew and vent
Your outrage
On all that is evil
Until the fire is spent.

When only embers and ashes are left
Let the cool, calm of God
Bring you peace.

LET ME BE ANGRY

When I am angry
About my abuse
I don't want to hear nice thoughts
From you.

Let me rant and rave
Over what was done to me,
Or what I was made to do.

I need empathy, not advice.
Sit and listen, with sympathy.
What happened to me
Can never be minimized.
Even God is outraged!

I don't need to hear
That God will make it right,
That somehow even this
Will be used for my good,
that I will help others
Because of what I've endured.

Right now, in my anger,
I'm even angry at the God
Who can do all of that.

Don't tell me about healing
When I never wanted to be hurt!
Who asked me if I wanted to
Experience hell
So I could identify with others?

In fact, I'm "mad as hell,"
That I was "thrown to the wolves,"
Naked, exposed, used, unrescued.

Nobody came,
Nobody cared.
And where was the God then
who wants to heal me now?

Just let me be angry.

AUTHOR'S COMMENTS

Some of the traumas of your childhood may seem shocking and unbelievable to you, as the Lord reveals them. There seems to be no end to the evil and human degradation that the enemy perpetrates on little ones. It is appropriate to let yourself feel outrage and anger as you become aware of what was done to you. It is only safe now, in the present, to feel the victimization and violation of self. It wasn't safe when you were little, for the punishment would have been great.

Don't be frightened by the intensity of your feelings. They will cool as you touch the depth of the pain and share your ordeal with a caring person. An understanding person will not try to talk you out of your feelings. Your anger will abate naturally, as you fully embrace the pain, finally accept your abuse, and release it to the Lord.

THOUGHTS TO JOURNAL

• Have you sensed you have anger inside, but have been afraid to touch it?

• What do you think would happen if you did feel how angry you are?

• Do you think God could handle your feelings of anger, even toward Him?

• God honors righteous anger. What has happened to you that has been unrighteous, unfair, and wrong?

• Can you see the difference between the perpetrator and the evil forces operating through that person?

• When you are ready, can you forgive those who have harmed you?

PRAYER

Dear Lord,

Right now I'm just angry. Part of me is even angry at you God. But I believe you still love me and will help me sort this all out. My abuse gives me a glimpse of how horrible evil is. When I'm done ranting and raving, let me realize that you, Jesus, were unjustly tortured and abused. Let me hold on to the hope that your death and resurrection conquered the enemy, sin, and death. Please don't let me be stuck in my anger. Let me feel, grieve, and release it all to you.

I WON'T FORGET YOU

Please don't be afraid.
I won't forget you.

Now that I'm getting stronger,
Now that I am healing
And not as shocked
At the memories you hold,

I can listen to
Your little heart,
The part of me
That quietly left
So long ago.

When I think of what
You suffered all alone,
I cry.

Do you see my tears?
They fall as a memorial
To your pain.
Let them tell you that
You are not forgotten.

One day this healing process
Will all be over.
It will be behind us.
I will know what you know
And we will come to acceptance
Together.

I know you are there.
I know you exist
And I know when you're ready,
We'll meet.

But for now when you feel me grieving
Over your leaving,
When my tears fall over your pain.
Just know you
Are not forgotten.

We will meet again.

I KNOW YOU EXIST

I know you exist, my little ones,
Don't run away.
Will you please come?
Will you please stay
In my conscious memory?

I'm not going to walk away
And leave you behind, this time.

I hear your cry, I feel your pain.
Could we be reunited once again?

You've been in the secret place of hiding,
Lost in trauma too great to endure.
I want to find you.
I know there's more.

I know you exist.
We can work together now.
I want you out alive.
With love and care
You will begin to thrive.

GIVE ME TRUTH

Lord, would you give me truth?
So much is still
Unknown, untouched
Hidden from me
From my conscious memory.

I desire truth in my
Innermost being.
Is there something I believe
That holds back memories,
Keeping me disconnected
From myself?

Yet sometimes I feel
The burning pain
Of wounded parts
Seeking life again.

Help me find the beliefs I hold
That guard and protect
My secrets.

Are my guarded beliefs
Barring the door of entry
Into trauma past,
Still locked away?

Even if I believe I will die
If I allow myself to remember my abuse,
You, Lord will tell me the truth.

You say, "It's safe now to remember,
That I did live and didn't die,
That you are with me, I survived."

Then I will know
What I have hidden,
Not wanting to be revealed.

My mind will hear, "It's safe to know"
And then I can be healed.

CAN I KNOW

How deep can I go?
How deep can I know
In my "not knowing"?

What forgotten memories, events
Are still hidden behind
The protective curtain I erected
That believes "I cannot know."

Lord Jesus, please
Give me courage
To pull back the veil
Of "not knowing".

I am ready.
I choose to know
What my mind believes about my knowing
All that's behind
My conscious awareness.

Give me strength to look
At my beliefs,
To bring them to light.
I ask you Jesus to reveal the truth
So we can make it right.

Let me see.
What I believe.
I can know.
You can show me truth.
And in that truth I will find
I can look deep within my mind.

Then I can feel, grieve
And comfort my wounded self.
I can release and forgive
My tormenters.

And you, Lord Jesus,
Will right all wrongs,
Wash my soul
Heal my heart,
Make me whole.

Soon all will be remembered,
All fixed,
All integrated,
All free
Walking into freedom,
Stepping into me.

AUTHOR'S COMMENTS

The human brain is designed by God to separate, split or fragment itself from the emotions and memory of abuse and trauma in the early years of life. When the child is unable to comprehend what is happening to him or her in a situation of extreme conflict in his or her limited understanding, there can be immediate forgetting, or dissociation of the event. This early ability to dissociate is intended to be a release valve, so the rest of the child's reality is not blown and the mind destroyed.

Unfortunately for some children, dissociation becomes a way of life, handling all intolerable situations by not remaining consciously present. Other children go on to learn healthy coping skills, and have no conscious recall of their traumas.

When a soul is fragmented, each fragment can hold a part or the whole of the memory and emotions. These fragments are locked into the time frame of the original event. The memories become "lost" to the conscious mind because the brain does a disconnect due to the overwhelming trauma. The memory is segmented from recall. The child unconsciously begins to believe that the abuse is too horrible to recall, or too dangerous to know or tell. The child may be threatened with death if they talk. The choice to not remember then holds the abuse away from the conscious mind.

However, memories can be triggered into consciousness in an adult's life through events, dreams or body memories. It can be frightening to discover past events or dissociated parts of oneself, and difficult to accept their reality. The fragmentation affects the adult, even when he or she is unaware of the source.

The Lord wants to heal your soul by helping you accept the reality of your trauma. He will bring integration through your processing what was once hidden.

THOUGHTS TO JOURNAL

• Do I have disturbing dreams?

• Do I have memories of my younger years?

• Do I sometimes react to things in an emotion or manner that is unlike me?

• Do I lose time? Do I often lose or misplace things?

• What do I believe would happen if I remembered my abuse?

• Ask Jesus about that belief, or beliefs and if they still hold true.

PRAYER

Dear Lord,

Where I am broken, I am willing to consider any beliefs about how I would feel if I remembered. Please bring your truth to any lies I may be telling myself. Help me listen to my inner self and not reject or deny any memories I may have through dreams or recall. Lord, I desire truth in my innermost being. With your strength and mercy helping me, I can know all my history and come to healing resolution.

UNPROTECTED

Out the door.
Big world, little me.
No rules, no training,
No boundaries given,
No restrictions...
Unprotected.

But I was smart,
Independent,
Naive, unknowing...
Unprotected.

I wasn't given rules of safety:
Where to be cautious,
When to say "no,"
"Walk with others,"
"Tell us where you're going,"

What is good touch, bad touch,
Bad promises, wrong secrets,
And always, "You're allowed to tell."

I didn't know these things,
But I was smart.
I could figure it out.
I could take care of myself.

But I did know a few things:
Be nice, say "yes", be polite,
   Trust grown-ups,
Respect your elders,
Protect your elders.

And when those elders
   Didn't protect you,
I knew you didn't tell.

Because I was sweet,
   I was nice,
   I was naïve...
I was unprotected.

LEAVE ME ALONE

Leave me alone!
Go away!
I don't want to see you!
I don't want to see anyone!

I like being alone,
No one around,
I can do what I want.

No interruptions, no requirements,
No demands.
Just me - all alone,
Safe, content.

Nobody looking,
Nobody requiring,
Nobody judging.

Leave me alone.
I can't take care of you.
Go away.
I only have room for me
Right now.

I like to hide, disappear,
Find a little space,
A little place, hidden,
Dark and quiet
Where I'm alone
And nobody can find me.

I don't want to interact, be social,
keep you happy, pretend.

Sometimes I'm not nice
And you don't have to understand.

Just go away
Leave me alone
And I am safe.

LIVE AGAIN

How does cracked dry ground
Receive rain?

How does a crusted-over
Hardened heart
Receive love?

Too much, too fast
Flows over the surface
And the life-giving source
Is not absorbed, but lost.

My emotions are so dry
My heart so empty
My thirst so deep.

Is it safe to receive?
Is it right to need
What seems to flow
So naturally in others?

I learned long ago
That soft hearts
Yielded and tender to receive
Are made fools
By those who betray a sacred trust.

Lord, only you can heal and restore
A shriveled heart.
Your gentle, soft and tender rain
Begins to bring new life again.

Softly, tenderly, you call me
Out of shame,
Out of the lie that love is not to be,
That I cannot receive,
That others don't care, aren't there
For me.

You will protect me, Jesus.
You are safe.
You give me people who love and care.
You and they are there
To gently rain love on a dry and thirsty heart
So I can live again.

HE'S NOT YOUR DADDY

The man in your life
That you see every day
That eats and sleeps
And lives in your house
Is not your daddy.

The grown-up part of you
Made a commitment
To this man to invite him
Into your heart and life
As long as you both shall live.

Your daddy is gone.
He died when you were young.
There was much brokenness
Between the two of you
And there was not enough
Time to heal.

All your unresolved anger,
Your critical thoughts,
Your frustrations, disappointments,
And hurts
Are stirred by this man
In your house.
But he's not your daddy.

If only you could shape
This man
Into the daddy you needed,
Then your raging pain could be healed
And you would find peace.

But no matter how hard you try
To change this man
In all your little girl ways,
Nothing seems to work
And nothing gets healed

Because he's not your daddy.

RESCUED FROM LOVES ILLUSIONS

It felt so free.
So intoxicatingly wonderful,
So addictingly insane
In this magnetic relationship
That drew us together.

It was beyond the mind to comprehend,
So powerfully driven,
So magnificently experienced.
I wanted to tell the world
Of my new found love.

But for all the joy bursting to be free
There was the nagging reminder
That our relationship
Could never be or exist
In the real world.

We could never tell the wonder
Of our discovery.
We could never share with others
The joy of our times together.

For they were secret, hidden, stolen,
Apart from the truth,
That neither of us were free
To be together.

The agony of experiencing one world
While living in another
Was only temporarily soothed by times together.

At night we went home to different beds
And had to live divided lives
With internal secrets ripping my heart.

But God came to rescue me
From my insanity.
His true love was stronger than my illusions.

He called me to repentance
And healed my shame-filled heart.
Now I know real freedom,
Been given a brand new start.

It's no secret.
I can tell the world abroad
I've been delivered,

By my wonderful God.

TRYING TO MAKE IT RIGHT

Can someone inside explain
Why I was drawn from the
Safety of marriage to open my
Heart to another man?

"I can tell," a little girl part spoke.
"I tried to make it right.
I gave your heart to an older man
You trusted, to whom you went for help,
Hoping to work out your yet
Unknown abuse."

"I projected onto him
The persona of the original man you trusted.
Like him, this other man was intelligent, enjoyed your
company
And showed you attention."

"I thought this time
My trust would be honored.
I could pour out my affection
And cute girlish ways,
And he would just delight in me
Like it was supposed to be
With the original hurtful man."

"Like all little girls,
I wooed and pursued his heart.
He was my hero, I his little princess.
And when this projected man
Responded with sexual touch
It made me feel good to be so loved."

"Now I could make the abuse of long ago
Turn out right this time around
So there would be no pain and shame."

"But wrong is wrong.
No matter how hard I tried
To make it feel right in this time frame
There still was only pain and shame."

"The cycle of betrayal continued
And now enlarged
To harm more innocent victims than myself."

"I'm so sorry.
Please forgive me.
I was only trying to make it right."

AUTHOR'S COMMENTS

There is an unconscious drive inside us to fix what is broken. Hemfeld, Minerth and Meyer in their book *Love is a Choice*, call it "Repetition Compulsion." If your childhood was painful, it is very likely you are setting up your adult life to re-play the pain in some familiar way. You are attracted to people that seem familiar, even if the familiar is hurtful. The unidentified drive or compulsion is to have another try at the original dysfunction, but this time to make it turn out differently.

Your attempt to finally heal the relationship between you and Daddy or Mommy never works if you are doing this in your marriage. You are no longer a little girl or boy, and your husband or wife is not your Daddy or Mommy. You may even find you are assigning a parental role to employers or friends.

This repetition compulsion can also explain why some people are ecstatically drawn, against all moral sanity and reason, toward a person outside their marriage. A younger part of themselves wants to play out an earlier drama, expecting in some illogical way that the pain coming from the past will be comforted and the original dysfunctional or abusive relationship mended.

As you accept the important people in your adult life for who they truly are, and not for who you project on them to be, you can learn what needs to change in you to heal the situation, not trying to change the other person who can never make up for your wounded childhood.

THOUGHTS TO JOURNAL

• Have I set the stage of my adult life to look like my childhood?

• Who do my significant others remind me of from my past?
(This could be positive or negative or a mixture, but it's
important to separate them from who they remind you of.)

• Am I using childish ways to relate, or try to change people?

• What adult skills can I use to help my relationships that I
didn't possess as a child?

PRAYER

Dear Lord,

*Please help me see where my adult pain is triggered by unhealed
childhood pains. Will you come to my child part and comfort what
was never comforted? Will you listen to my cries for help when no
one came, and show me your caring heart? Help me to forgive all
the adults who failed me in one way or another when I was little.*

*Protect me from temptation triggered by past wounds. Keep me
from isolating in anger and withdrawal. Show me my responsibility
in bringing healing to my present situation. Bring me to safe and
loving people where I can be healed.*

CONFLICTED

Jesus, you created my body
To enjoy sexual feelings.
You designed me so that when
My private, special place was
Rubbed, touched, caressed,
I would feel pleasure.

I was created to enjoy my sexual self,
To gladly open my body, mind, and soul
To a man who loved me exclusively
And cared for me tenderly.

Your plan was for this man
To be my husband,
The one I entered into covenant with you
To remain true
For life
And freely give myself
To him.

But, Jesus, your original, perfect plan
For husband and my sexual delight
Was distorted, robbed, by lustful men
Who grabbed their pleasure
While destroying mine.

I learned to cut off long ago
All flow
Of pleasurable response of body touch
And even now in the place of safety
With a loving husband.

And when I do desire pleasure
My mind would only permit me
To think illicit, wrongful thoughts
To connect with body touch for release.

I am conflicted, Lord.
My brain has wrongly trained my sexual expression
To only live through shame
To gain
A rightful desire.

DISCONNECTED

"My job is to help you
Not feel sexual pleasure,"
Says a part of me.

"You knew it was not right
When you were being wrongly touched,
And when your body responded with pleasure
You felt such shame."

"I came to your rescue
And severed the pleasure
From the touch.
I shut down your brain
When it was happening again."

"I vowed you would never
Let a man pleasure you sexually.
This way you won't have to
Feel the guilt and shame
Of enjoyment."

"Because of me you could tolerate
The unwanted touch
That came secretly at night."

"I won't let your body respond.
You lay stiff, straight and silent
And soon it was over."

"It was harder after you were married,
But I kept you from believing the truth -
That you were sincerely loved
And enjoyed."

"This way you didn't have to feel your body
And connect with the shameful emotion
Or memory
That you were abused."

"It's my job.
I keep you disconnected.
I keep you safe."

DISCOVERING MY DISCONNECTOR

I am beginning to find
Parts of me, of my mind
That have taken on
A life of their own.

For so many years
I didn't know
I had an inner self
Who worked to keep me safe
From sex.

I often wondered
About the lack of interest,
Awkwardness and pleasurelessness
Of marital sex.

Yes, sex is part of marriage,
And it's only right to allow
My husband to enjoy me,
But it didn't mean I had
To partake.

My Disconnector was
Silently doing her job,
Keeping me shut down,
Keeping me safe.

There were ways I learned to
Override her, push her aside,
So I could feel my body
And the pleasure of response.

But I was not proud
Of my bag of mental tricks,
For the sadness it brought to my spirit,
Just so I could participate in enjoying
What the Lord had naturally intended for pleasure.

It is with surprise, and relief
I find my Disconnector.
So much conflict and confusion
Have begun to relieve.

Can we work together now?
I desire to receive
All God's intended delight

TO MY DISCONNECTOR

Thank you for a job well done.
Now that I know what you do
And why you came
I am grateful you sabotaged their game.

You kept me safe from the shame
Of feeling sexual pleasure
Wrongly solicited.

My not feeling
Was the only thing I could control.
I couldn't stop the visits at night
But I didn't have to feel
Or respond to the touch.

The abuse was shameful
But you kept me from
The deeper shame of responding
With enjoyment.

Now that I'm remembering my abuse
Your job makes perfect sense.
You were right to disconnect my body
From my emotions.

But now I need your help
To change my brain
To help me feel again
The Lord's intended pleasure
In sexual intimacy.

Hear the truth , this part of me.
I am now safe in a Godly marriage.
It is the Lord's purpose
For us to desire and enjoy sexual union.

I choose to trust.
I choose to freely give all of me,
Body, soul, and spirit
To the man I love.
It is right, good, and honorable
To experience the pleasures of sex.

Now your job is to be my Reconnector.
We will feel. We will heal. We will be free
To love and enjoy
All God originally planned
When he gave me my man.

INTIMACY LOST

A young child
Does not have concerns
Over body image and sex.

But through the years
If there is betrayal, wrong touch,
Words and acts of sexual violation,
They collect themselves
Into building blocks of beliefs.

Over time an attitude
Of how we perceive self and sex
Is formed and directs
Our thoughts and life.

The blocks of thoughts
Placed strategically in our mind
By the enemy causes us to believe
We are soiled, shameful, unlovable.

A young bride
Finding true love, marries,
And brings to the marriage bed
Her past, her thoughts, her pain.

"I don't deserve to feel
the Godly pleasure of my body,"
she reasons.
"I cannot trust my heart to any man."
"I will give my body, but not my heart."
"I will keep myself safe
By not being present."

And so an unfulfilled
And divided life is established,
And God's heart weeps
Over the intimate joy of marriage
That is lost.

INTIMACY RESTORED

I see, I care, says God,
Over the robbery of my gift
Of marital sexual pleasure.

How dare the enemy
Plant seeds of violation
In the garden of my
Precious little one, God cries.

These seeds grow weeds
That cover the heart
And crowd out thoughts
That sex is pure and good
According to my original intent
Between a man and a woman.

I created a bride
To experience Godly passion
Toward the man of her dreams.

I gave her a body equipped
To be responsive, expressive,
Uninhibited and passionate.

Come to me, my precious bride.
Show me your soiled garden of broken trust.
Let me help you pull each lying weed
That says you cannot
Experience my gift of intimate oneness
And pleasure.

I will soften your garden grounds
With my love and my waters of truth and life.
Together we will uproot lying beliefs caused by betrayal,
And destroy the deep roots of abuse.

There is no woundedness
So deep that I cannot heal.
I will plant flowers of hope
And trust and healing.

I will restore intimacy lost.
I will bring you to your husband
Clean and pure.

Experience all the pleasures of sexual passion.
Delight in the joy of fully participating
In intimacy restored.

AUTHOR'S COMMENTS

One of the saddest, longest-lasting fall-outs of sexual abuse, even after it is over, is the sexual response of the victim. You may become sexually promiscuous, or the opposite, sexually shut down.

Much of the healing must take place in your brain. What are you believing about yourself and about sexual expression? What defenses have you learned to cope with because of the unwanted sexual abuse early in your life? You can either believe that since you have now been sexualized, you will just keep it up, and somehow take pleasure in using others as your victims. Or you can protect yourself from anything sexual.

More often, the aftermath of abuse appears in the sexually safe environment of marriage. Your brain may have learned to cut off pleasure. You may have made vows to yourself to "not feel." You don't give yourself permission to respond to loving, sensual touch. Sadly, you may even believe your husband is not loving and sincere in enjoying your body. You don't believe you can trust any man.

THOUGHTS TO JOURNAL

• Which way have I responded to sexual abuse?

• What do I think about when making love?

• Do I have to picture ungodly images to be aroused?

• Do I give my husband/wife my body, but not my heart, when we make love?

PRAYER

Dear Lord,

Please heal my damaged sexual responses because of my abuse. I reject and break all vows I made, conscious or unconscious, to "not feel sexual pleasure." I forgive and release my abusers. Show me how to trust my husband and believe he has my best interest in mind when we are sexual. Help me yield myself, body and soul to him, that we may both enjoy your intended pleasure for us. Help me be responsive and passionate as you have designed and blessed in the covenant of marriage.

I'M SO ASHAMED

I'm so ashamed.
I hang my head
And feel the dread
Of having failed.

I've disappointed those I love
And who knows what
My God above
Must think.

I'm bad.
I'm naughty.
Stand in a corner,
Sit on a chair,
Should have known better,
Not sure why I'm there.

"Time Out" is up,
Yet not forgiven.
Just pretend it's OK
And go on living.

"I'll be perfect,"
I vow,
Though I don't know how.
I just need to be loved
But I feel so ashamed.

I hang my head
And feel the dread.

Imperfect, unwanted,
I know I've failed.
Can't make it right,
Feel no love.

Just know somehow,
I need a hug.

YOU'RE NOT PERFECT

My precious little one,
You've been lied to.
You've held on to a belief
That is not from me, your Lord.

Somehow you believed if you could
Do everything the way others required,
Then you would be accepted and loved.

You believed if you didn't measure-up
You were a disgrace, a failure.
The shame of imperfection
Drove you harder to try to please
To ease the pain
And receive the love.

Some people even wanted you to believe
That I, your loving Father God,
Would only love you if you followed
All the rules.
The more perfect you were,
The more I, the Lord, would love you.

Please, hear my heart, when I tell you
"You're not perfect – and
In this life you never will be."

Take that rigid rule off your heart
And accept your humanity.
Relax and do your best to love and please,
But not to ease guilt and earn acceptance,
For I've already and always have been loving you,
Completely.

More…

Let me remove the shame of your false belief
Of striving to be perfect
In order to be loved.

When things happened to you over which you had no choice,
It did not make you less lovable in my eyes.

I know too well how sin tries to destroy,
But your being soiled – as a victim or by choice,
Never, ever, changed my heart
Toward you.

I know you're not perfect.
Accept the truth.
You can be imperfect,
Even soiled,
And still be loved.

It is imperfect, fallen, soiled people
That I came to save.
I wash you clean and give you a new heart
That can grow to be like mine.

Let's look at the truth together,
Knowing, no matter what happened,
How messy and imperfect it was,
No matter how much you feel you failed,
It will never stop my love.

I love you always, forever,
My precious, dear,
Imperfect Daughter.

FAILURE AND SHAME

"To err is human,"
It has been said.
But somehow
Inside my heart and head,

I believed that
I was supposed to be
Above being human
And behave in a way
That proved I was special,
Superior,
Better than others.

So when my world of denial,
Carefully built
To sustain perfection
Came crashing down
With the truth of sin and abuse,
I was pierced by shame.

My God in Heaven, have mercy,
Forgive me for my false beliefs.
I accept my failure.
Forgive me for believing
I had to be
Perfect.

REDEEMED – NOT PERFECT

Can you accept
That you were never perfect?
I loved you, God says
From the moment you were conceived,
But even then, you were imperfect.

The ritual abuse
Just added to the brokenness
You already carried.

Your ancestors were deceived
Into believing they had
Hidden knowledge
To make themselves superior,
And use the uninformed.

They rejected the Truth
Of their own sin.
They chose knowledge
To be "like God"
And make themselves perfect
Rather than seeking to be
Reconciled to their Creator
Through the redeeming blood
Of my Son.

Blood became important in rituals,
Mocking the true and only legitimate blood sacrifice
Of Christ.
You were baptized into false blood
And endured perverse ceremonies
To make you become one of them.

More...

But my love pursued you
Drawing you out of deception,
Breaking through the defenses,
Reaching the brokenness of your wounded soul.

I have been loving you
Out of generational, ancestral, and personal deception
Into the Truth of
True reality.

I am not ashamed of your imperfection
And the damage of ritual, sexual abuse.
Sin is sin.

*All sin
Has it's consequences.
Yet all sin
And even sin's consequences
Are redeemable
By the blood of Jesus Christ.*

*It is my Son's joy to redeem and restore
Once imperfect you.*

*And now, as my redeemed one,
He presents you faultless
And with great joy,
Before me, your Father,*

Perfect.

NOTHING TO PROVE

My dear one.
You have nothing to prove
To get my attention,
To achieve my love,
To make me want you,
And to call you special.

Being "good" and "the best"
Will not impress me
To love you more
Than I already do.

You don't have to prove
You can behave perfectly
And never fail,
Because of the false belief
That it's the only way to be loved
And special.

You already <u>are</u> special
And you must accept
You are human.
I knew there would be failures,
I knew you would sometimes make bad choices.

But I am a Good Parent.
I do not condemn, but forgive and love.
As you seek my help and direction
I teach you to grow
And learn from consequences.

Your failures become bridges
To better choices.
There is no shame here,
Only gain.

As I forgive you
You forgive yourself.
I am so proud of how you are
Growing, recovering, and healing.

My heart is moved.
You are special and dearly loved.
You have nothing to prove.

FAILURE IS NOT A SHAME

My Child, I hear your cry.
You no longer need to deny
You are human.

And like all humans,
You will believe things untrue
And behave in ways unfitting
For you.

You know I sent my Son
To save you from sin.
I never expected you to be perfect,
Apart from him.

Therefore you can rejoice,
You are redeemed.
Your sins are forgiven
Your abuse cleaned.

Your failure is not a shame.
It's only the enemy's game
To condemn and
Wound you further.

Look into my eyes
See my love, hear the truth,
I'm not ashamed of you.

Cast your feelings and failures,
Your experience and situations
On me.

I will take them from you
And carry you through
To healing and wholeness.

I love you always.

I'M NOT ASHAMED OF YOU

Dearest child of mine,
I see your pain
I feel your shame.

Let me lift your
Hanging head
And tell you
You are loved.

I'm not ashamed of you.
I know what you've been through.
I've forgiven,
Made provision
For you to know my love.

Let Jesus hold you,
Enfold you in his care.
He is there.

Lift your downcast eyes
To see the love in mine.
Your heart must know
You are loved by me.

What I say is true,
I'm not ashamed of you.

There is no sin so wrong
No abuse so deep
No failure so great
That my love is not
Deeper still.

For a season, the enemy used and abused you.
You were deceived and believed his lies.
But I have rescued you.
For now, and all eternity,
You are mine.

You are forgiven, cleansed,
Rightly dress as the princess you are.
No more sorrow, no more pain.
No more shameful living.
Jesus has died
So full redemption can be given.

Safe in his arms, knowing it's true
I've never been ashamed of you.

AUTHOR'S COMMENTS

Shame is such a strong and powerful emotion. If your shame is tied into trying to be "perfect" so you could be loved, it carries even greater shame and pain of imperfection. It is very hard to try and maintain the belief that you had a "perfect" childhood if you knew you were soiled by abuse. And if you believed your acceptance was based on "being good", you knew you have failed. If you still carry deep scars of feeling dirty and unlovable due to early abuse, it is normal to feel imperfect. The only way to maintain an image of perfection is to deny that anything ever went wrong.

Even if you were not abused, realizing that God has never held you to a "perfect" standard can help you accept the truth that you are loved for who you are, not for what you do or what was done to you. You join the human race when you can admit you are also human. It is such a relief to realize you are loved for just being you, human and all.

THOUGHTS TO JOURNAL

• What causes me to feel ashamed?

• Have I tried to be "perfect" so I would be more accepted and loved?

• Can I believe that God loves me for who I am?

• Have I asked God to redeem me from my own sin and any sin perpetrated upon me?

PRAYER

Dear Lord,

Forgive me for believing I could only be loved by you and others by trying to be good. I humble myself before you and admit I have failed. I give you all my shame and feelings of unworthiness. Thank you that you have made provision for all my sins and failures, and even for those who have sinned against me. I forgive those who harmed me and release them to you for judgment. Come into my life, Lord Jesus, and cleanse me of all unrighteousness. Heal my broken heart and soul and fill me with your love.

I CAN'T ACCEPT TRUTH

Is it pride, or shame
That keeps me playing this game
Of not accepting truth?

Our family had high standards.
We thought we were to be models
For others to follow.

We lived a Christian life,
A "looking good" family
Where everyone was perfect and nice.

I knew I was to be a good example,
A cut above the rest.
I was to do things well
And learn to excel.

It just couldn't be true that a model little girl
Could be badly soiled,
For who would she be if she was imperfect?

From failure comes shame.
Shame has more pain than pride.
Shame is about who I am
When I'm unable to be perfect.

"Shame on you," was often used
To remind me to have pride
And keep the family stride.

To know I've failed
And feel the horrifying shame
Of imperfection
Makes it impossible for me
To look at truth.

I would not be able to exist
If my abuse was true.
My failure would be so great
I could never be perfect,
My shame so great,
With truth I would not survive.

I am locked in unbelief by shame and pride.
How can I accept truth?

I'M STUCK

My mind is stuck
In confusion.
Tossed to and fro.
What's yes, what's no.

Was I really abused?
Did these things really happen
To me?
Who would ever do such things
To a sweet little girl?

Yet I have enough memories,
Feelings, tears and dreams
That point to inevitable truth
That "Yes, it's true.
These things did happen to you."

My protection of total amnesia
Is gone,
But enough disbelief lingers
To make me question.

Perhaps I can just clean it up, justify,
Minimize the memories
So they're not really
That bad.

That way I can hold on to my need
To not really be damaged,
Soiled, or imperfect.

There is such shame to fully accept
That if this really happened,
My own and my family's image
Would be ruined, you see,
And it would be because of me.

So it's safer to stay stuck
Between denial and acceptance.
I can still pretend it's
"Not that bad,"
And keep some dignity that
"I'm not that soiled."

IF I ACCEPT TRUTH

There is no healing
In staying stuck.
If there is to be wholeness
I must step into truth.

What if I did say it's true -
That I was abused,
Betrayed by a loved one,
Involved in sexual rituals,
Dedicated to false gods,
And totally split off all memories
Into dissociated parts?

If I accepted truth
I would have to feel the shame
Of all this horror happening to me,
That my family had dark secrets,
And I now have dissociated parts.

Would that mean I'm a freak,
Or am I actually innocent?
Did I want it to happen, make it to happen,
Or was I a victim?

What will others think of me
If I admit the truth?
Will I be judged, thought less of,
Isolated, feared, thought weird?

Dear Lord, help me.
I don't want to stay stuck,
Yet if I accept the truth,
Will I still be loveable?

Will you love me? Will I love myself?
Can I ever be proud of me again?

Jesus, you said you are the Truth.
Help me step into you
And choose to know the truth of my reality.

You saw it all.
Give me the courage to receive the truth
I don't yet know.
I believe you will show me what I need to know,
And I can trust in you.

JESUS IS NOT ASHAMED

Jesus is not ashamed
Of what was done to me
Or what I chose to do.

He is not ashamed of me
That I failed to be perfect,
That I was damaged by abuse,
That I've "let him down,"
That I've failed others,
That I've failed myself.

He is not ashamed
That I didn't measure up
To other's expectations,
That I've been insensitive,
Trampled on other's feelings,
Unaware of other's needs,
Ignorant of my behaviors
And how they impacted
Those I loved.

Jesus is not ashamed
That I failed my own expectations
And lived in the denial
That I was perfect
For fear of shame
Destroying me.

Jesus is not ashamed
Of my shame.
He is not ashamed
That I never knew what I did wrong,
And if I hurt others with what I did
I was too ashamed to look at my guilt
And apologize.

He is not ashamed of me
Hiding inside for shame,
And returning when I could pretend "all is well."

He has seen it all
And loves me still.
He took all my guilt and shame
To the cross.

I've been made clean,
Guilt and shame are washed away.
This is the dawning
Of a brand new day.

TRUTH AND SHAME

Truth is
I was damaged, soiled, broken,
Used, abused
And my innocence taken.

Any hope of being perfect
Was dashed, destroyed.
I could never return
To unsoiled innocence,
Sweet and pure.

Jesus tells me this is true.
Not only could I never return to unsoiled,
But I needed to grieve the truth,
That I was never truly
Sweet and pure,
Yet to know even then,
I was always loved by him.

Jesus tells me he is Truth,
And long ago
Man was deceived, and started to believe
Lies planted by the enemy.

I carried in me the same deception
Of my generations and family system.
We believed we were not deceived,
But rather more perfect than others.
We were here to help and fix
Those who didn't know how.

Stepping into occult, hidden knowledge
Was believed to exalt the family line
With power and superiority.
All failure would be shame.

More...

But the Truth is
Neither my family nor I were ever superior.
Truth tells us all have sinned.
I too, like all, was born already damaged,
And then damaged further
By occult ceremonies and rituals.

I carried false shame
Over my imperfection
And I continued the protection
Of those who hid in the occult.

They believed the lying deception
That their abuse to me
Was making me into a superior being.

Yet the Truth is
I was not superior.
I was a victim.
All the shame is on the perpetrators.
It belongs to them,
Not the child.

The rituals were shaming to me,
But I was not the ritual.
The shame was never mine.

Jesus rescued me.
The shame was washed away.
Humbly before him now
All my pain I lay.

NEVER MY SHAME

Jesus, I pray, forgive me for believing
And holding on to the enemy's lies.
I accept my sin
And imperfection from the beginning.
I accept you as my Savior.
I accept your blood sacrifice
Cleansing me of all unrighteousness.

The ritual, sexual ceremonies
Were never my shame.
I no longer need to deny the truth
That these things happened to me.

I accept I am imperfect
And it's human to fail.
I have been shamed
But no longer hold the blame.

I can accept Truth,
Sorting it all out,
Grieving, releasing, and forgiving,
Being forgiven, loved, and accepted.

I can walk in Truth.
I am redeemed.
Jesus has made me truly sweet and pure
And innocent.

His Truth has made me free.

AUTHOR'S COMMENTS

If you were raised with the false belief system that your behavior was more important than you, that any approval you received was based on your performance, it is very common to struggle with shame. You learn to "keep face" by seeking others' approval and putting on a false sense of pride. It is very painful to let go of the protection of pride that helps you have some sense of importance.

If there was emotional, physical, or sexual abuse in your family of origin, you may be stuck in the denial of protecting the family image, as well as your own image and sense of value. You still believe appearance and performance are what make you acceptable.

When you can honestly tell a trusted counselor or friend your beliefs of failure and the truth of your story, you begin the road to freedom. You find you are not judged, you no longer need to protect someone else's behavior, you can be real and grieve your losses. You no longer need to cover up the pain you have been carrying.

When you realize you are loved, no matter what was done to you or what you have done, you can be free of the tormenting shame. You no longer need to hide behind pride and perfection.

You forgive others, you forgive yourself, and begin to walk in authentic sense of your own value. You believe the truth that God loves you and has made provision for your true redemption.

THOUGHTS TO JOURNAL

• In what ways was I valued as a child?

• What do I believe makes me important?

• What is the true story of my childhood? Have I shared this truth with someone?

• Can I accept that Jesus loves me and is not ashamed of me? Why or why not?

• Consider writing a forgiveness "letter" to all who have hurt you. (Between you and God) "Dear…This is what you did to me…this is how it made me feel…I choose to forgive you." This letter can be destroyed, or if desired, a kinder version mailed. If the person is now dead, you can still write the forgiveness letter. We are free to forgive, regardless of the other person's attitude. (Jesus on cross.)

PRAYER

Dear Lord,

Help me to accept the truth that my value comes from you, and that you love me and will never leave me. Please forgive me of all my sins of wrong beliefs about you, about me. Forgive me for all my ways that have not honored you. I invite you to be the Lord and Savior of my life. Wash me clean and make me a new person. I forgive all those who have sinned against me, just as you have so graciously forgiven me. Forgive me, on my part, for holding judgment and hate. Heal my wounded soul and let me walk in new freedom and love, healthy and whole.

I HAVE ALWAYS LOVED YOU

I loved you when you were
Imperfect.
I loved you and wept over you
When you were being sinned against.

I have always loved you
And will never stop loving you.

I pursued you in so many ways –
Through beauty and wonder of creation,
Through kindness and love of others,
Through awe of worship
And joy in service.

You are wonderfully and uniquely
Created by me.
I have perfectly designed you
To be the very person you are becoming.

Even perpetrated, evil deeds
And tragic events,
Cannot destroy you.
I am partnering with you
In overcoming their effects.

Know the Truth that I am
A Good God
And would never harm you.

More...

When all is said and done
We rejoice together
That you are the beautiful, intended one,
Who has not only survived,
But has overcome.

You have overcome the enemy's plan
To destroy you
And to keep you from me.

The enemy is defeated.
You are finishing the race
and the destiny I've set before you.
You are victorious.

You shine with the light of Truth
And my redeeming love
And life within you.

As your Heavenly Daddy,
And your Creator,
You bring me such joy.

I have always loved you.
I love you now,
And I will never stop loving you.

We will love each other together,
Always, and for all eternity.

Precious one,
I love you!

About The Author

Trudy Colflesh has had a tender heart and sensitive spirit since childhood. She grew up in the home of a Presbyterian minister and saw her parents seek to meet others' needs in Christian love and service.

Trudy became active in service herself in high school and college. She graduated from the College of Wooster, Ohio, married her college sweetheart and worked several years in a Presbyterian church as a Director of Christian Education.

For many years, Trudy was a stay-at-home mom and active in volunteer church service. She and her husband, George, have two natural children, Christopher and Karen, a son Michael, adopted when he was ten years old, and have fostered two young boys.

When Karen was almost seven, she became ill with leukemia and despite doing all possible to save her, she died within seven months. Out of this painful time, Trudy wrote the book *Too Precious To Die* and traveled around the country speaking at Women's Aglow Fellowships and appearing on CBN and other TV and radio programs.

Having opportunity to minister to hurting people, as she herself was healing, Trudy felt the Lord calling her to go into the field of counseling. She went to graduate school and earned her Master's degree in Counseling at Montclair State University, New Jersey, in 1990 and became a Licensed Professional Counselor.

Since that time, Trudy has worked as a Christian Counselor, ministering hope and healing to countless clients. She has listened to her own soul cry and pursued recovery, as well as listened to the hearts of her clients. She knows with certainty, that out of the painful issues of life, comes a sure belief that Jesus Christ knows our emotional pain, hears our soul cry and brings us His Presence to comfort and heal.

"And we know that in all things God works for the good of those who love him, who have been called according to his purpose." (Romans 8:28)

Trudy is available for telephone counseling and coaching. If you would like to set up an appointment, please contact her at Trudy@Encouraginghope.com. Comments or questions may also be addressed to Trudy at this location.

SEE OTHER BOOKS IN THE SOULCRY SERIES

Book 1
Shame, Confusion, Numbness, Escape, Anger,
Loneliness, Lostness

Book 2
Abandonment, Emotional Wounding, Relationships,
Fear, Sadness, Rejection

Book 3
Enmeshment, Identity, Pain, Inadequacy, Shame,
Dependency, Dissociation

Book 4
Sexual Abuse, Denial, Ritual Abuse, Dissociation,
Betrayal, Control, Identity, Trauma

Book 5
Dissociation, Suffering, Ritual Abuse, Sexual Abuse,
Forgiveness, Comfort, Healing, Joy

Book 7
Denial, Worth, Dissociation, Ritual Abuse, Rejection, Sexual Abuse, Surrender, Love, Healing

Book 8
Enmeshment, Attachment, Self Worth, Suffering, Occult Bondage, Generational Iniquities, Mercy, Freedom, Integration

Book 9
Denial, Guilt, Shame, Lost Identity, Lost Time, Reputation, Dissociation, Programming, Comfort, Safety, Original Self

All books are available to order at:
**www.encouraginghope.com/soulcry
Amazon: Go to Trudy Colflesh books**

Too Precious To Die

Seven year old Karen Colflesh was diagnosed with AML, Acute Myelomonocytic Leukemia, a rare form of the disease not usually found in children.

Too Precious To Die, is an intimate, personal account of Karen's battle against this deadly disease. It is as triumphant as it is tragic.

Karen's courageous fight was an inspiration to all who came in contact with her.

This story shows the victories the Lord God won on Karen's behalf, and the healing miracles He demonstrated throughout her illness.

However, despite all the doctor's skill and the faith of many, Karen was called home to Heaven in a glorious vision.

Trudy shares how she and the family overcame their grief and found answers and comfort to Karen's early death.

Trudy has shared Karen's story throughout the country, speaking at Women's Aglow meetings, as well as on radio and TV.

She and her husband George were guests of Pat Robinson on the 700 Club.

This is a moving, compelling story that draws the reader into the experience. *(paperback, 248 pages)*